P9-CED-624

GRASSLAND ECOSYSTEMS

by Melissa Higgins

Content Consultant
Sara G. Baer
Professor, Department of Plant Biology
Southern Illinois University

Core Library

An Imprint of Abdo Publishing
abdopublishing.com

abdopublishing.com

Published by Abdo Publishing, a division of ABDO, PO Box 398166, Minneapolis, Minnesota 55439. Copyright © 2016 by Abdo Consulting Group, Inc. International copyrights reserved in all countries. No part of this book may be reproduced in any form without written permission from the publisher. Core Library™ is a trademark and logo of Abdo Publishing.

Printed in the United States of America, North Mankato, Minnesota
042015
092015

THIS BOOK CONTAINS
RECYCLED MATERIALS

Cover Photo: iStockphoto
Interior Photos: iStockphoto, 1, 4, 8, 22, 24 (top), 24 (top right), 24 (middle), 24 (bottom left), 24 (bottom right), 26, 31, 34, 40, 43, 45; Shutterstock Images, 10, 24 (middle top), 28; Steve Geer/iStockphoto, 14; Suzanne Tucker/Shutterstock Images, 16; Lynn Bystrom/iStockphoto, 19; Jason R. Warren/iStockphoto, 24 (top left); James Tung/iStockphoto, 36; Chris Crafter/iStockphoto, 38

Editor: Jon Westmark
Series Designer: Becky Daum

Library of Congress Control Number: 2015931039

Cataloging-in-Publication Data
Higgins, Melissa.
 Grassland ecosystems / Melissa Higgins.
   p. cm. -- (Ecosystems of the world)
Includes bibliographical references and index.
ISBN 978-1-62403-854-9
1. Grassland ecology--Juvenile literature.   2. Grasslands--Juvenile literature.
I. Title.
577.4--dc23
                                                              2015931039

CONTENTS

CHAPTER ONE

WHAT IS A GRASSLAND?

A mouse hurries through dry stalks of grass. It is looking for its favorite seeds. A hawk coasts overhead looking for its favorite meal—the mouse. The hawk dives to the ground. It snatches the mouse in its claws and flies away. The hawk carries the mouse to its hungry chicks.

Thousands of miles away, a lightning bolt hits dry grass. Flames shoot across the countryside. Gazelles,

Red-tailed hawks circle over grasslands looking for movement on the ground.

hedgehogs, and cranes scurry or fly to safety. Underground, grass roots are not harmed. They will spring new growth when rain comes.

Around the World

Grasslands exist on every continent except Antarctica. This ecosystem covers approximately 40 percent of Earth's land surface. All of the grasslands in the world have one thing in common—grass is their most common plant.

Grasslands are known by different names around the world. In North America, most grasslands are called Great Plains. In Africa they are known as savannas or velds. Most grasslands in Eastern Europe and Asia are called steppes. Grasslands in South America are

And the Winner Is . . .

Australia is the country with the biggest percentage of land covered with grasslands. Approximately 70 percent of Australia is grasslands. Forty-two percent of China is covered with grasslands. Grasslands cover 37 percent of Russia, 36 percent of the United States, and 32 percent of Canada.

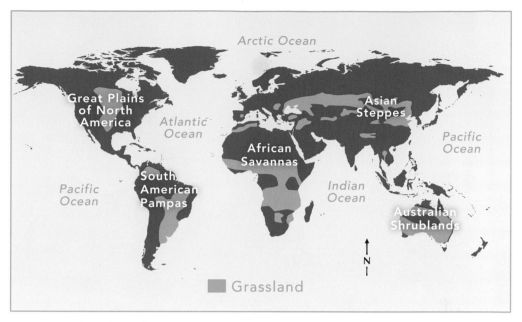

Grasslands of the World

This map shows grasslands across the world. Sometimes a picture is easier to understand than reading words. In two sentences, explain if looking at this map or reading the text of Chapter One helps you better understand where grasslands are located.

called pampas, llanos, or cerrados. Most Australian grasslands are known as shrublands.

Grasslands are diverse ecosystems. This means they contain many different kinds of plants and animals. Some of the biggest animals on the planet live in grasslands. Grasslands contain hundreds of types of grasses and other plants, such as wildflowers. A healthy grassland ecosystem contains a delicate

African elephants are the world's largest land animals. Habitat loss is one reason they are endangered.

balance between its plants, animals, and the environment.

Important Yesterday and Today

In the past, many grasslands were larger and had more wild animals than they do today. Over time, people began to grow crops. They also learned how to raise animals for food. Farming and grazing took over much of the world's grasslands. Many other grasslands were destroyed when towns and cities were built on them.

But grasslands continue to be important ecosystems. Land that was once grassland is now farmland that provides food for much of the world. Surviving grasslands attract tourists and are used for recreation. Grasslands help limit global warming. They are one of the most important ecosystems on Earth.

Helping the Environment

Factories and automobiles put a large amount of a gas called carbon dioxide into the air. Like the glass covering a greenhouse, carbon dioxide traps heat. This makes the world warmer. Grasslands help fight global warming. Grassland plants take up carbon dioxide into their leaves and use it to make roots. This removes the gas from the air. Scientists are looking for ways to make grassland plants store even more carbon dioxide.

CHAPTER TWO

GRASSLAND CLIMATE AND WEATHER

Grasslands can be divided into two main types: tropical and temperate. Most tropical grasslands are located in the southern hemisphere. They cover large areas of Africa, South America, and Australia. Temperate grasslands are found mostly in the northern hemisphere in North America and Eurasia.

Maned wolves have long legs that help them see over the tall grass of tropical cerrados.

Scientists also sort grasslands by how much moisture is in the air. A lack of moisture is called aridity. Scientists classify grasslands using six aridity zones: cold (the driest zone), hyperarid, arid, semiarid, dry subhumid, and humid.

Tropical grasslands are mostly semiarid or humid. Summer brings 28 to 56 inches (71–142 cm) of rain to tropical grasslands. The grasses in these areas can grow very tall because they get so much rain. Some grow up to seven feet (2 m) tall. The dry season lasts for two to seven months. Tropical grasslands do not get much colder than 64 degrees Fahrenheit (18°C), even in the dry winter months.

Temperate grasslands are mostly arid and

Rain Shadows

A rain shadow is an area of very dry land that is blocked from moisture by a mountain range. Rain shadows can create dry grasslands. The western portion of the Great Plains in the United States sits in the rain shadow of the Rocky Mountains. As a result, this region only supports shorter grasses.

semiarid. Rainfall ranges from 10 to 30 inches (25–100 cm) per year in these areas. Grasses in the temperate region tend to be shorter because they get less rain than tropical grasslands. The driest temperate grasslands are the western short-grass prairies of the United States and Canada. The tallgrass prairies in the eastern parts of these two countries get more rain. Grasses here can grow very tall if they are not grazed. Temperatures in temperate grasslands can vary from below freezing in winter to more than 100 degrees Fahrenheit (38°C) in summer.

EXPLORE ONLINE

The focus of Chapter Two is the climate and temperature of grasslands. The website also discusses these things. As you know, every source is different. What information on the website is the same as the information in Chapter Two? What are the differences? What else can you learn about grasslands from the website?

The Grassland Biome
mycorelibrary.com/grassland-ecosystems

CHAPTER THREE

GRASSLAND PLANTS

Plants play an important role in grasslands. Grasses have a large root system that anchors them to the ground. This keeps the soil in place. When plants die and decay, they return nutrients to the soil. This makes the soil richer. Plants also bring energy into the ecosystem. They combine the energy from sunlight with carbon dioxide and water to make sugar. Sugar provides food for plants to grow. This

Prairie sunflowers turn to follow the sun to take in more light.

Forbs are common in grasslands. They often have colorful flowers.

process is known as photosynthesis. When an animal eats a plant, the plant's energy transfers to the animal. This allows the animal to grow.

Native Plants

The most common plant in grasslands is grass. But grasslands can contain hundreds of different plant species. There are approximately 10,000 types of grass in the world today. In the United States, common prairie grasses include blue grama, big bluestem, wheatgrass, and buffalo grass. All grasses have slender leaves, called blades.

Sedges, rushes, and other grasslike plants grow in grasslands. Forbs and a few types of woody plants can also grow in grasslands. Forbs tend to have wider leaves than grass and often produce showy flowers. Forbs include globe mallow, sunflower, coneflower, and black-eyed Susan. Trees and shrubs are woody plants. Not many woody plants are found in healthy grasslands. Fires are common in thriving grasslands. The blazes burn woody plants before they can grow too large.

Buffalo Grass

Buffalo grass is one of the most important plants of the US short-grass prairie. Pronghorn, rabbits, and prairie dogs graze on it. It was once the main source of food for the huge herds of bison that roamed the prairie. The burs on buffalo grass seeds cling to animal fur. They drop off the animal in new places and grow into plants. Buffalo grass roots can grow five feet (1.5 m) deep in the soil. The grass is resistant to heat and cold because of its deep root system.

Grassland plants have adapted to grow well in their environment. Grasses and forbs have developed deep roots. These roots are not harmed by fire and can reach moisture deep underground. Grasses' long, slender leaves have a small area for the sun to shine on. This keeps them from losing too much water. Forbs hold their broad leaves upright to avoid too much sunlight. Both grasses and forbs have low growing points. This means that the part of the plant that makes new cells is close to the ground, protected from grazing animals. Many

More Plant Species than the Tropics

Tropical ecosystems have more plant species across large areas than any other ecosystem—as many as 942 plant species per 2.5 acres (1 ha). But in 2012, a team of biologists measured the number of plants in smaller spaces. In these places, grasslands had more plant species than any other ecosystem. A 527-square-foot (49-sq-m) patch of grassland in the Czech Republic contained 131 plant species. A 10-square-foot (0.1-sq-m) area of grassland in Romania had 43 plant species.

Some nonnative species, such as Canada thistle, spread their seeds by sticking to animals and people.

grassland plants can go dormant. This helps them survive harsh conditions.

Nonnative Plants

Plants introduced to an ecosystem where they do not usually grow are called nonnative plants. These plants might be brought to an area accidentally. They can be carried by wind, animals, or people. Nonnative plants are not often affected by the same weather conditions, diseases, and insects that help keep native plants in check. So nonnative plants can quickly overtake a natural grassland habitat. One study looked at plants in the Pawnee National Grasslands in eastern Colorado. Out of 410 plants, 70 were nonnative. These plants take space and resources away from native plants.

Humans may bring nonnative plants to an area for a specific reason, such as for farming. Rich soils make grasslands some of the best farmlands on Earth. Grasslands tend be flat. This makes them easy to farm. Many parts of the world that were once native grasslands are now used for growing food. The US prairie, for example, is one of the richest farming regions on Earth. Crops, such as corn, soybeans, cotton, and wheat, have replaced many native grassland plants in the United States.

Fire and Grazing

Fire, both natural and man-made, is important to grasslands. Fires destroy trees and shrubs that might overtake grasslands. Fire burns away layers of dead plant material. This provides more light for grassland plants to regrow.

Grazing animals are also important to grasslands. Like fire, grazing opens up areas of soil to more light. It reduces the height and density of grasses, making room for shorter plants to grow. This can help grasslands become more diverse. But grazing can be harmful to native plants. If animals are kept in a single area for too long, they can eat too much of the grass. Overgrazing hurts plant and soil health because plants do not have a chance to fully grow. This can open up areas for nonnative plants to enter.

FURTHER EVIDENCE

Chapter Three provides information about grassland plants and some of the factors that help and hinder healthy grasslands. What was one of the chapter's main points? Go to the website below. Find a quote from the website that supports one of the chapter's main points. Does the quote support an existing piece of evidence, or does it add a new one?

Grassland Ecosystems Profile
mycorelibrary.com/grassland-ecosystems

CHAPTER FOUR

GRASSLAND ANIMALS

Animals are important to grasslands in many ways. Prairie dogs, for example, prune the plants they eat. Their droppings make the soil more fertile. Their burrows provide homes for many other small animals. And small animals provide food for grassland predators.

In the past, grasslands stretched unbroken for hundreds of miles. There were herds of millions

Prairie dog holes provide shelter for other burrowing animals and make the soil more fertile.

Grassland Food Web

This illustration shows a typical grassland food web. The arrows show the movement of energy through the ecosystem. In what ways is the information in the diagram the same or different from the information described in Chapter Four?

of wild animals. There are fewer wild animals in grasslands today. In some areas, food crops are planted where wild grasses once grew. Domesticated animals compete with wild animals for food and space. But grassland animals are still as diverse and interesting as those found in any ecosystem.

Grazers and Predators

Some grassland animals eat only plants. They are called herbivores. These animals take in energy plants have created through photosynthesis. Examples of tropical grassland herbivores are elephants, gazelles, zebras, and giraffes. Antelope, bison, jackrabbits, and prairie dogs are herbivores that live in temperate grasslands.

The Last Bison

Scientists estimate that up to 30 million bison once roamed the Great Plains. In the early to mid-1800s, the governments of Canada and the United States decided to develop the Great Plains for farming and ranching. This decision led to the mass killing of bison. The animal was almost wiped out. The last free-roaming bison were killed in the United States in 1891. Bison today live in nature preserves, parks, and zoos, as well as on private land.

Monarch caterpillars eat milkweed for approximately two weeks until they are fully grown. They then begin the process of becoming a butterfly.

Some animals eat only meat. They are called carnivores. Lions, hyenas, leopards, and cheetahs are carnivores in tropical grasslands. Bobcats, wolves, snakes, owls, and hawks are carnivores in temperate grasslands.

Omnivores eat both plants and other animals. Jackals, warthogs, ostriches, and baboons are omnivores in tropical grasslands. Temperate grasslands are home to omnivores such as raccoons, coyotes, foxes, and various bird species.

Insects

Insects are the most abundant and diverse group of animals in grasslands. Insects are very important to grasslands. Some insects, such as bees, pollinate plants. This allows plants to make seeds that grow into new plants. Other insects, such as dung beetles, help break down dead plant and animal material. This creates rich soil for plants and helps clear the ground for new growth. Grasslands, in turn, provide a home for insects to thrive. Grasshoppers, bees, beetles, and ants live in both tropical and temperate grasslands. These insects provide food for many birds and small mammals.

All grassland animals play a part in this ecosystem. They each help balance the system to ensure its continuing survival.

Butterfly and Milkweed

Two natives of the prairie, the monarch butterfly and the milkweed plant, depend on each other. Milkweed produces a bad-tasting poison that keeps most insects from eating it. But the poison does not hurt the monarch. When it is a caterpillar, the monarch eats only milkweed. The poison builds up in its body. This makes the caterpillar poisonous to birds. In turn the butterfly pollinates the milkweed. This helps ensure its survival.

CHAPTER FIVE

PEOPLE AND GRASSLANDS

People have lived in grassland ecosystems throughout human history. In fact the earliest people may have lived on African savannas. Over time, human activity has changed grasslands. But people today still depend on grasslands for their food and livelihood.

Many people still rely on grasslands to feed their herds of animals.

Fragmented Grasslands

Fragmentation happens when a large ecosystem is separated into small sections. People split up grasslands by building roads and cities, as well as planting crops. Fragmentation makes it harder for fire to spread. It also makes more edges. Edges are places where grasslands border other types of land. Edges can let trees, shrubs, and nonnative species find their way onto grasslands. Native grassland animals have a harder time finding mates and food in small grassland patches. Fragmentation can lead plants and animals to go extinct.

Spears to Plows

Early humans gathered native grassland plants for food and medicine. They hunted large grazing animals, eating their meat and using their hides for clothing and shelter. Hunters knew they had better chances of finding game on healthier grasslands. They set fire to grasslands to keep them free of shrubs and trees. Burning also extended grasslands into larger areas.

Approximately 11,000 years ago, humans began to grow crops from grass

Land fragmentation and farming hurt grassland habitats.

grains. They started raising cattle for food. Humans
eventually began to rely less on hunting and gathering
and more on farming. This change reduced grasslands
all over the world. People plowed grasslands to grow
crops. Tamed animals were kept in small areas, where
they overgrazed grasslands.

With an abundance of food produced with
the help of grassland soil, the human population
grew. People built towns and cities on grasslands.
They began preventing fires instead of using fires
to manage grasslands. Large grasslands were split

into smaller sections. Animals that needed larger habitats could not survive in these smaller areas. Their populations fell.

People and Grasslands Today

People still depend on grasslands today. They eat meat and dairy products from animals raised on grasslands. People hunt native grassland animals for food. Crops, such as wheat, corn, and soybeans, are grown on grasslands. They are used to feed most of the people of the world.

Grasslands provide other opportunities, such as hiking, hunting, and nature viewing. For example, tourists enjoy seeing the elephants, lions, and giraffes of the African savanna. Tourism can help visitors understand and respect grasslands.

Some people use grasslands as their ancestors did. On the Mongolian steppe, for example, early people moved their sheep and yak herds around grasslands for good grazing. Some people living in this part of the world still do this today.

This US Geological Survey (USGS) press release from 2001 discusses the dangers fragmented grasslands pose to nesting birds:

> As grassland areas are divided into smaller tracts of land, there are more "edges" and fewer large, open grassland areas for birds to nest in. . . . From 1998 through 2000, USGS biologist Rosalind Renfrew and her colleagues . . . placed miniature cameras at 89 nests of five grassland bird species in southwestern Wisconsin pastures. They found that most of the bird predators were raccoons, thirteen-lined ground squirrels, and snakes. About one-third of the nest failures were caused by species that prefer the woody edges of grasslands, such as raccoons and opossums, and these nests were usually closer to woody edges than other types of edges.
>
> Source: Rebecca Phipps. "Grassland Birds and Habitat Fragmentation: The Role of Predators." USGS Newsroom. *US Geological Survey*, August 5, 2001. Web. Accessed February 24, 2015.

What's the Big Idea?

Take a close look at this passage. What is the main connection being made between land fragmentation and bird population? What can you tell about the relationship between bird nests and grassland edges?

CHAPTER SIX

THE FUTURE OF GRASSLANDS

All of the parts of a healthy grassland ecosystem support one another. So problems with one part can cause problems with others. For example, a sudden loss of coyotes or badgers due to overhunting could cause the number of prairie dogs to rise. When there are too many prairie dogs, grassland plants may be overgrazed. Having fewer plants could cause soil to erode and weeds to spread.

Coyotes help control the population of burrowing animals, such as prairie dogs.

As human populations grow, more grasslands are being developed for human use.

There are many threats to the world's grasslands. Most threats are a result of human activity, such as urban growth. Urban areas continue to cut into grasslands. But humans are taking action to save these important ecosystems.

Threats to Grasslands

Crop production is one of the biggest threats to native grasslands. Native grasslands are continually being converted to farmland. Poor farming methods, such as growing only one type of crop year after year on the same soil, increase the chances of pests and disease. Pests and disease increase the need for chemicals and substances that protect crops. These things can be toxic to native plants and wildlife.

Nonnative animals threaten native grasslands. Cattle can harm grasslands if there are too many of the animals in too small of an area. They overgraze and erode the soil. Nonnative plants may grow in overgrazed areas. Once nonnative plants start growing, they quickly reproduce and compete with native plants. Nonnative plants are often not as nutritious as native plants. As a result, native grassland animals have a harder time thriving.

Black-Footed Ferrets

The black-footed ferret is a type of weasel native to the Great Plains. It was once thought to be extinct. Over the past 30 years, state governments, federal agencies, zoos, conservation groups, Native-American tribes, and landowners have helped bring the ferret back to its native grasslands. Today there are almost 1,000 black-footed ferrets in North America. The animal is still endangered. But its recovery shows that the prairies where it lives are healthy.

Habitat loss and hunting have hurt African lion numbers.

There are other threats to grasslands too. One example is climate change. Climate change can vary the amount of rainfall an area receives. Too much rain can cause flooding and erosion in grasslands.

Fire suppression is another concern for grasslands. For a long time, people have tried to stop the spread of fire in these ecosystems. As a result, trees and shrubs have taken over some grasslands.

Because of hunting, there are fewer big grazing animals, such as elephants and zebras, living on the

African grasslands. Hunting also has reduced the number of predators, such as lions and cheetahs.

Helping Grasslands

People are taking action to preserve grasslands. This can be as simple as getting rid of trees and shrubs and setting fires in the dry season. Some areas need more work. This might include planting native seeds and reintroducing native animals.

Establishing national parks helps protect grasslands. Two grassland national parks include Theodore Roosevelt National Park in North Dakota and Grasslands National Park in Saskatchewan, Canada.

Many countries have passed laws against hunting endangered

Biofuel

Some native grasses are being used in Europe and North America as an energy source. Switchgrass, buffalo grass, tall fescue, and canary grass can be grown in poor soil. These grasses are changed into a liquid fuel. The fuel can be used to make heat and electricity. It also can be used in place of gasoline for some cars and trucks.

One way people help protect grasslands is by starting and controlling fires.

animals. Farmers help grasslands by letting soil rest between planting crops or by restoring grasslands on formerly cultivated soil. Ranchers help grasslands by moving their livestock to new locations to keep them from overgrazing.

In the past, people often protected grasslands. In return, grasslands provided them with food, clothing, and shelter. Today people are beginning to understand grasslands are too valuable to lose. They are trying to find new ways to protect them.

President Theodore Roosevelt began as a rancher in North Dakota in the 1880s. During that time, he witnessed the prairie grasslands being ruined. He created the US Forest Service to protect wildlife. In his 1913 article "Our Vanishing Wild Life," he wrote:

> [I]t is also vandalism wantonly to destroy or permit the destruction of what is beautiful in nature, whether it be a cliff, a forest, or a species of mammal or bird. Here in the United States we turn our rivers and streams into sewers and dumping-grounds, we pollute the air, we destroy forests, and exterminate fishes, birds and mammals—not to speak of vulgarizing charming landscapes with hideous advertisements. But at last it looks as if our people were awakening.

Source: Theodore Roosevelt. "Our Vanishing Wild Life."
Theodore Roosevelt and Conservation. *National Park Service*, February 22, 2015.
Web. Accessed February 24, 2015.

Back It Up

Roosevelt used harsh words to describe what was being done to the environment. But he ended his article on a note of hope. Write a paragraph describing at least three pieces of evidence from Chapter Six showing how countries can help grassland plants and animals.

WELL-KNOWN GRASSLANDS

Great Plains of North America

The Great Plains of North America are located in the United States and Canada. Almost 90 percent of this temperate grassland ecosystem has been converted to farmland and cities. This is more than any other grasslands in the world. Some of the best-known mammals of the Great Plains of North America are bison, coyotes, and prairie dogs.

South American Pampas, Llanos, and Cerrados

The South American grasslands are located in the southern half of South America. They are found in Argentina, Brazil, Bolivia, Paraguay, Uruguay, and a small part of Chile. More than 75 percent of the South American tropical grasslands are now used for farming and ranching. Jaguars, maned wolves, giant armadillos, and giant anteaters live here.

Central Eurasian Steppes

The temperate steppes range from northeastern China westward through parts of Russia to the Ural Mountains. Only about 20 percent of this grassland ecosystem has been converted to cities and farmland. Wild animals, such as the Mongolian gazelle, hedgehogs, marmots, and several species of crane, share the land with domesticated sheep, yaks, and goats.

The shape of their feet enables the kangaroos of the Australian shrubland to move around by hopping.

African Savannas

The African savanna spreads through 27 countries. More than 73 percent of these grasslands still remain. The savannas are home to some of the best-known animals on the planet. Elephants, giraffes, lions, zebras, rhinoceros, and wildebeest call this ecosystem home. One of the world's most famous national parks, the Serengeti, has the largest number of wild grazing animals and predators in Africa.

Australian Shrubland

Australia has more of its land covered in grasslands than any other continent. Approximately 57 percent of its grasslands have not been converted to cities or farmland. Australia does not have large herds of animals as Africa does. But kangaroos, wallabies, dingos, wild pigs, ravens, eagles, and rabbits all live on Australia's shrubland.

STOP AND THINK

Take a Stand

This book explores how some grasslands are being lost to agriculture. Which do you think is more important, preserving grasslands or expanding farmland? Or do you think both are important? Write a short essay explaining your opinion. Make sure to give reasons for your opinion and facts and details to support those reasons.

Tell the Tale

Chapter Five discusses the first humans who lived in grasslands. Write 200 words telling the story of a hunter living on the Great Plains of North America 2,000 years ago. What animal species does he hunt? What types of plants does he gather? What is the hunter thinking about? Describe the sights and sounds of the grasslands. Be sure to set the scene, develop a sequence of events, and offer a conclusion.

Why Do I Care?

Think about the foods you eat and the clothes you wear. How many of them come from plants or animals that live in grassland ecosystems? What if grassland plants and animals no longer existed? How would your life be different? Are there things you would miss? What are they?

Surprise Me

Think about what you learned from this book. Which two or three facts did you find most surprising? Write a short paragraph about each fact describing what you found surprising and why.

GLOSSARY

adaption
a change in a population over time

aridity
a measure of how much an area lacks moisture

diverse
showing a great deal of variety

domesticated
tamed or grown by humans

dormant
not actively growing but able to begin growing again

endangered
in danger of becoming extinct

extinct
no longer existing

forb
a flowering herb

graze
to eat small amounts of food throughout the day

sedge
a grass-like plant that grows in wet ground or near water

species
a group of living beings that are similar to one another

LEARN MORE

Books

Latham, Donna. *Savannas and Grasslands*. White River Junction, VT: Nomad Press, 2011.

Patkau, Karen. *Who Needs a Prairie? A Grassland Ecosystem*. Toronto: Tundra Books, 2014.

Roumanis, Alexis. *Grasslands*. New York: AV2 by Weigl, 2015.

Websites

To learn more about Ecosystems of the World, visit **booklinks.abdopublishing.com**. These links are routinely monitored and updated to provide the most current information available.

Visit **mycorelibrary.com** for free additional tools for teachers and students.

INDEX

ABOUT THE AUTHOR

Melissa Higgins writes fiction and nonfiction for children and young adults. When she's not writing, Higgins enjoys hiking and taking photographs in the Arizona desert, where she lives with her husband.